# The Fourth Symphony

# I would not have been if you had not existed

Nadia Abu Shama

Dr. M. E. Fayad

# Brilliant Stars in the Sky of Literature and Writing

My sophisticated erudite student, Nadia Abu Shama, is of Algerian origin. She is a distinguished writer, an eloquent first-class person, and a talented writer. In a fantasy world other than that one you live, you are under a spell with her charming words, dancing with her messages. She is able to stir up all the sorrows confined in your deep recesses, so as to perceive the universe with the eyes of purity, serenity, and childish ecstasy.

She was born and brought up in the Babur Mountains - the city hanging at the foot of a large mountain with a geographical and historical heritage and home to revolutionaries during the French occupation, where great revolutions and battles took place. This region of enchanting and rare beauty was very isolated and remote from the capital city , just like a pearl or an expensive diamond concealed from all the world's eyes.

Collaborating with Dr. Fayyad, she has written thoughts, in the form of letters, and more than forty books, "Universal Symphonies." Examples of her masterpieces are: "The Novel of Al-Taffar" , "The Nude Body," "The Legend," "Dancing on Water," "The Ram Dancer," "The Gazelle of Al-Bawadi," "The Prisoner of the Past," and "The Rape of a Woman".

0000000

Dr. Muhammad Fayyad, an American of Egyptian origin, spent more than forty years, dedicating his life to the niche of knowledge, and spending the best days of his life in fruitful scientific research. Then generations, graduated under his supervision and sponsorship, believed in the value of science and learning, which contributed indirectly to the renaissance and development of America and other countries of the world through multiple expeditionary trips to spread knowledge around the globe.

Dr. Muhammad Fayyad contributed positively and globally to raising the status of human civilization in the world and participated in composing the "Cosmic Symphonies". Among his scientific, literary and reform works, he published ten scientific and permanent books and more than 500 scientific articles in the most famous scientific journals and conferences. And add to this, his striving to spread his innovations in the "Engineering of Unified Concepts", "the Unified and Stable Linguistic Engineering", "the Engineering of the Unified Field", and "the Art of Abstraction" . This is all with God's help.

# Dedication

*To the one that I no longer meet and desire to confess to her that without her I am destitute and lost.*

*To the one that I lost, so my soul with her was lost.*

*My life is no longer my life.*

*To the one that made me follow her in the scent of distinguished women's perfumes, and search for her in their faces and run after her eyes so that I might find the sparkle of her eyes.*

*To the one that made me meet all the women in search of her angelic face.*

*To the one who left me with no return...*

**Nadia Abu Shama**

I walked alone on the road, my soul.

I have been searching for my soul for years,

...and I am still searching.

**Dr. M.E. Fayad**

# Table Of Contents

# 1

# The Vacant Pillow

How long the nights are without you!

How miserable they are when fantasies haunt me!

When I find the strong scent of your body filling my room!

When I find the pillow on which you are supposed to lay your head crying out because of your frequent absence!

When I find the bed creaks as your body has not been thrown on it for a long time like a quarrelsome child!

The bed creaks as it has not embraced you like the homeland embracing a new foreigner!

Your perfume bottles would breathe deeply because for a long time you did not put them on your fragrant body!

I did not put them on in my hands to pass them on your face after shaving!

Your silk pajamas, folded in the bed corner, are cold as winter and severe frost.

They could not leave their place as every night they are waiting for you.

Everything in the room would stone me so that I might miss you more.

I could throw myself into the paws of eagerness for you.

How much I loved my life before I knew you because I was like the Alaskans at the frozen pole.

I was not tempted by nightgowns in the shops.

And I didn't make my bed and fumigate my room and put all my adornments.

I was just staying up to hit the books or surfing the internet pages.

I was then smiling at every lover and his confessions.

Before I knew you, neither my ribs nor my heart was trembling. I was not struggling with your fantasies. The deadly desire to meet you did not attract me.

I feel that I am a woman who is exempt from love and its stories.

My heart was not created to shiver at the foot of your name or at the first gleam of you.

I wouldn't make up a language or a message to sail to you through it every day, or make it like a paper boat which children make.

My room and everything in it reveals to me my longing for you and always reminds me of my being alone with you.

Oh how much I love you!

How much I stumble and fear my stuttering in front of you! How ashamed I am of all my ribs that tremble only when your name is mentioned!

When night falls upon me!

I want to travel... yes travel to a country where there is no love within the dictionary of life.

I would like to live in very distant islands where your imaginations or breath cannot reach me, or your body smell fights me.

Tell me that you love me, even if only a lie, so that my night will calm down... and my bed will rejoice, and the tears of your pillow close to me will dry.

Tell me that you will contain me, and you will return to your home with me so that darkness will dissipate in my depths, so that I can regain my freshness and beauty.

Just tell me that you love me so that the smell of your body can subside and I forget the burning of your eagerness, in order to change the balconies of my house.

Tell me that you love me so that I can travel away from you and live in other realms.

Be sure, if it was easy for me to fall in love with someone else, I would have run to the first man I met on my way, just to forget you.

Just to forget my burning every day, to escape your being lonely with me every night.

I do not like you to break my ribs when you embrace me because you are like me as well.

I do not like you to pour into my lips the fire of your longings that inhabit you and set the tongues of flames of your eagerness within me to force me to submit and melt in you.

I do not like to melt in your arms.

I do not want to be a flame that burns within you.

I do not like to be with you for one day or one hour.

Do not hug me tightly and pull me to you because I do not want our time to end after an hour or half an hour.

And then you leave for all your labors and be away for months and years.

I want to be free from you, because I am like a piece of silk between your palms, slipping and sliding where I do not know where to fall.

I want you to gather everything you have in my room and leave, because I can no longer bear the smell of your body, nor your distance, nor my femininity rebelling in me.

I want to leave the home of your eyes and the contours of your lips that made my body its favorite geography, made the hills and borders of my body its path.

I want not to be your eagerness and longing as long as I am not alone in your life.

Collect all the fragments of your soul and the pains of your love that scatter within me and turn me into burning longings like grains of corn.

I burn like ears of wheat.

I love you and I do not desire your circle of silence that limits me and hides much of you from me, and forcibly distances me from you.

I fear that you will miss me one day when you are attached to me and love me madly, but you do not meet me. You do not find me. I fear that you will roam all places when you are moved by yearning, when you need my heartbeat and the dance of my days, when your soul sings my name.

Then you break your silence and shout at the top of your voice that you love me, that you want me, and that you search for me in all places.

5

# 2

# The inaccessible love

I miss hearing all the poems that you write secretly every night and hide in your inner pocket of your elegant jacket.

I miss all the words that you did not say to me and kept them imprisoned in your mouth.

You made them imprisoned in your breath, residing with your pains.

I am still waiting for another life, for you to confess to me, to lead me inside you and to inhabit the cities and streets of your eagerness.

I am still waiting for you to let me hear all the songs of lovers, and to dance with me like a movie star, like an extraordinary woman, like a constant eagerness within you, like your passion for love, country and freedom.

I am still waiting until I see your lips dancing when you remember me.

When I pass fleeting fantasies near you, I see all your images that I used to console myself with during the time of your absence.

I will cross a border where you are forbidden to be with me, where I am forbidden to love you deeply, passionately and with an audible voice.

For in my country my love for you is considered one of the great sins.

The detective will watch me and the leader will be angry with me.

The religious and social sects will revolt against me.

All the masses will attack me, and all your female lovers  will slander and stone me.

According to your traditions and ours, it is forbidden to declare love with a hopeful heart.

It is forbidden to love a rebel and a resister.

It is forbidden to love a miserable homeland, people, a cause, and a resistance.

It is forbidden to announce love, virgin and loyal.

That is why you always make up thousands of reasons and excuses for all our meetings so that we never meet.

In my country and yours, everything is permissible except love and doing good.

Everything is permissible for you except to admit openly that you love a resistance fighter, a patriot, or a poor person, because that is considered one of the greatest sins of time.

Speak about everything.

Acknowledge everything.

Unleash your potentials to everything.

Just don't take the reins out of your heart.

Don't let your strength seduce you, or admit that you loved or made good for the country and the people, for these sins are unforgivable...

# 3

# I am still waiting

When I dragged my steps like a handbag and headed to the first table on the Decabelage beach, I was filled with many hopes.

I thought I was like a colorful butterfly flying in all directions, indifferent to anything.

I sat on a chair facing the sea while I was sailing in its wonderful blue water, as if I were swimming in the fantasies of some teenagers who roamed the whole world with their pink dreams.

And she dances with all her glowing hopes. She chooses for herself what she wants from novels and movie heroes to search for them in her reality.

So, she wanders in all the roads and streets in search of the knight of her dreams.

The blue color of the sky and its serenity, the sea containing its smell, its salt, its waves, and its sound were all-encompassing.

I think I have left my consecutive and similar days that are torn apart by the daily routine.

Only today' s happiness was your date that you set for me, despite your busy agenda and interests, to the point that I did not believe that there was a date in the first place.

You often promised, but you often broke all promises.

I started dancing with the waves while the gulls were clapping their wings for me as they would gather on this beach that was distinguished by its virgin nature and its permanent calmness.

The waiter came and offered me a delicious glass of orange juice.

It does not matter if you are a little late because in any case you will come.

I thought of many years ago when I used to be alone with that sea and reveal all my secrets to it.

When I hid my pains in his closet like clothes for holidays, occasions and weddings.

How much he shared my joys and sorrows with me more than any other person, more than a lover whom I once thought was the one who would protect my weakness and prevent me from sorrows.

However, he was the one who made me a fireplace of passion and love that would sweep me away like a flood and would strip me of many wishes that were attached to my heart like stars in the sky.

If you ask the knowledgeable sea, it will tell you everything. Many wishes inside me have been broken, after which I no longer knew how to trust the heart and love.

After that I knew the insignificance of humanity and realized that what I was looking for was of no existence.

The most distinguished people in the world are of four categories: the first is an artist, the second is a genius scientist, the third is a leader, and the fourth is a fighter with a rebellious face.

I smiled with all my big dreams that I hid in the folds of the sea forever.

I smiled with all the stubbornness and might of my lovely eyes that were a powerful magic which would imprison all those who would see their sparkle.

After that I stopped their mischief, so I used to conceal them under the tufts of my hair to veil them from all people.

I crawled into my life fleeing from the history of my passions.

I forgot the table, the chair, and everything t surrounding me.

I only heard your heartbeat.

I used to smell your scent and the smell of your body that exceeded all the perfumes of the world.

The smell of your body was excelling all the perfume of Paris. Even if they were combined in one drop of perfume.

The smell would not change its color as if time had stopped twenty years ago, as if the Swiss watches stopped and no one could move them forward.

It is the same smell.

It is the same powerful odor, the same sound of your breath, the same loud laughter, and the same calm smile.

Oh, what a woman who has never known failure, who has never been defeated by continuous shocks or by refractions.

Distance does not draw boredom within her.

She always has fresh and strong energy within her.

The passage of time is neither slow nor fast.

Indeed, the time of the meeting has gone as fast as a train that waits for nobody.

You did not come.

I knew that I would always be alone because I chose you and did not choose anyone else, because you are my history, my dreams and hopes for the future.

I hate to live the ordinary time with the ordinary man.

That is why I always bear with you and all your contradictions.

I bear all the changes of life within you.

I bear all the zigzags that are folded in your days and your sequential time.

Since I knew you, I took off the watch from my wrist and got down all the watches hanging on the walls of my house.

When I came to see a clock in public places and in my office, I used to avoid it so that I do not know how much time and how many years you are absent from me.

How many promises you did not fulfill.

You promised me a lot to devote a lot of time to me soon.

Months and years passed by, and I did not know how you would measure time and history.

Is it by days, by years, decades, or centuries?

I don't know how you would count the years of your age or would calculate the time of your date with me.

I went down to the beach to walk on the sand and wet my feet in the waves of the sea, as I wet my cheeks with my burning tears.

I wish I could throw myself in your arms , so you would hold me tightly.

I wish I could hide myself in your passionate heart.

I wish you would wipe my tears, and never be late for me.

 I wanted you to contain me, because the most difficult moments for me are when I fight my fate alone, when I collect all my bags to travel to a capital city that I am not sure whether you love or not?

And do you like the land that I will make my home?

The land to which I, with my dispersed years,  will depart.

How much I wanted you to be near me as you always promised me, as I used to see it in the sparkle of your eyes.

Your hand often trembled when I intended to approach you.

You often heard my sad voice and words that come out of me like a musician who skips playing the strings of his lute.

Oh, what a pain that never leaves me or subsides within me.

Sometimes I wonder: How have longings moved you, and  how has eagerness burnt you?

How has love crucified you in its niche?

I wonder: How can you not be indifferent to all the dancing and constant pain of my heart?

How do you bury everything in your silence like the secrets of the resistance?

Time and hours moved roughly within me like giant waves escaping from the heart of the sea, throwing themseves on the shore, like a charming mistress throwing her graceful body on a smooth silky bed.

She is so seductive that no one can resist.

She looks at the eyes of her lover rushing to her like children rushing to pieces of chocolate and candies.

Today I was almost defeated, because I decided to change my destination, change my country, and change everything there.

For I don't know if I can meet you or not, because I don't know when and how we will meet?

I wanted you to be near me, to hold my hand, to whisper in my ear, to say goodbye to me at the airport, but you didn't and don't want to.

Oh, damn the times that separate between us like two parallel train raiways.

Oh, damn your silence, and damn your hesitation even though you can make me the mistress of the whole universe and make me a shining star.

You can make me a princess sitting on a royal throne.

You can confess to me everything that makes your heart crazy with love and moves you.

# 4

# I'm still dreaming

Every time I came to write to you, I would find myself out of breath, my energy would be gone, and an overwhelming fear would haunt me, as if I were taking an exam.

I would find all the words, I was supposed to write, were not the words I wanted to say.

I would find your love deeper and stronger than all the Arabic alphabets.

However, these are the letters of the language that God Almighty glorified and made it the language of the Noble Qur'an sent for the guidance of mankind.

 It was in itself a miracle throughout the ages, with its powerfulness, beauty, splendor, depth of meanings, and abundance of miraculous words.

I feel as if I was lost in front of a grand castle belonging to one of those chosen by God and distinguished with their special characteristics.

 Your heart is so wide and pure and that it loves in an extraordinary way, in a way that the rest of humanity has abandoned.

I love the classic ways of love, and I love the romance that we make all the time, the romance that is adorned with types of candles and various roses in many colors.

However, at the present time everything has become urgent and fast, even love has become for many people just like a take-away.

Then after that they complain about boredom, routine and emptiness.

They live only parts of their lives because the rest is all wasted with the speed of time.

They do not distinguish between a life of sophistication mixed with the real life of a person.

I still love and adore things in the typical way of love without any change.

Even the books that I love are classic, consisting of paper and black ink.

Their fragrant scent reaches my breath.

I adore them with all their alphabet.

I devour paper books as a smoker devours his addicted cigarette.

I still adore the earth, the rain, the sky, the greenery, the smell of the sweet soil.

I enjoy the birdsong.

I still run like children.

I still adore my grandmother's orchard and our garden.

I still dream and dream....

# 5

# My language of love

My language of love is not grasped by anyone but you.

No one will comprehend what I feel except you, my love.

I am not the only one who has been thirsty, but you and all people have been thirsty as well.

But most of them drink from cups other than their own and return to complain of loneliness and abandonment.

As for me, I have been looking for my real cup so that only you and I will drink from it, so that it will be for us alone, so that we can drink from it together, so that we can live our wonderful story together, so that we can tell each other that true love exists even in this current age.

I want to prove to the whole world that it is not only Nizar who found his love in his sweetheart Balqisah.

There are a lot of other lovers whose stories are much deeper and stronger than his in patience and endurance.

As for him, every moment of longing and every search trip inspired him to generate a beautiful poem.

His readers used to share his poems with him.

As for our case, we are the only ones who share everything.

We are the only ones who share happiness, longing and nostalgia, to say to all human beings that love has no limits.

It has no time to start, nor is it exclusive to a certain age.

It is true love that gives us our true ages.

It is the only thing that builds safe homes for us, full of tranquility, emotions and glowing longings.

It is love that draws everlasting happiness inside us.

It draws the desire inside us for each other.

The desire that continues as long as time and history goes on.

It purifies us from the things that have stuck to us and defiled us, and defiled the beautiful things within us.

Do not be surprised at the way I love you, because I am special, and I love excellence in everything.

I love to be alone with you throughout my life so that you may dwell in my gardens, and eat from my apple trees whatever you desire, because you will never get out of them.

I would have never been if you had not existed.

It does not matter how long you have been searching for me, how much time you have wasted to make your heart dance to the tune of my soul, because in the end you would find me exactly as I had found you.

Indeed, you were the best lover who wandered all around with me.

You sent into me flying spirits, like angels, that danced with me and ascended me from one sky to another.

You drove my breath to search for the scent of your fragrant body, for your silent heartbeat, for your glowing veins that would shine like stars, for the longing that would fill you.

Your love made me like the sping bride whose dress was always colored like the rainbow which the children love to see.

You made me frisk and spin like butterflies that cares about nothing in life except for happiness, pleasure, exhilaration and flight.

# 6

# O childlike poet sleeping in the depths of my beloved

O childlike poet sleeping in the depths of my beloved  were it not for you, I would not be sitting on the palace of his heart, and I would not be the queen of his soul.

 O childlike poet, you gave up writing poetry, but you did not know how to give up the beautiful language of love.

You could not give up the language of love buried inside you. You could not give up the childlike dream that you had, that inhabited your heart.

The abundance of your sense and your attachment to everything beautiful made me your favorite bride.

It made me the only female in your life.

You have engraved my image and my presence in your eyeballs, and on the walls of your heart.

You embraced me with the sparkle of your shining eyes.

You adorned me with ornaments and jewels from the shine of pleasure in your eyes.

You used to shape them for me into pieces of the utmost precision.

Then you put them on my entire beautiful body.

You enjoyed that as you used to dress me up in the garment of your love adorned with the threads of your wondrous love, after it was designed by my extreme love for you.

How wonderful it is to see the female herself a queen over all the thrones of her lover, to be a queen over all the homelands of his emotions!

She tries to bow before him in gratitude for what he gave her, because he gave her the authority over the palace of his heart.

He crowned her with his love studded with the jewels of his sincerity and passion.

So, she was free in all the world despite that his love for her is an ideal bond.

His love for her pushes her strongly to be the most beautiful woman on earth, to be the undisputed beauty of the universe, to be an ideal female in a time when palaces, crowns and queens have all disappeared.

In a time when the just sultan and the lover with all his powers, the beloved in every sense of the word, have never been found.

His love for her restored all the true meanings and synonyms of love.

His love for her pushed her to live again despite the arrows, daggers and swords that were embedded in her deep recesses.

7

# O My master! You are like a legend in the kingdom of love!

My master! You are like a legend in the kingdom of love.

I built it for you between my eyelashes.

You are like the sultan in the lands of my emotions and sacrifice.

You are completely free to live, to think, to plan, and to make decisions because you are the sultan of my just heart.

You contain me and provide me with everything you have.

You make of me a distinguished princess in whom your love grows as green fields grow.

Also, life thrives in you as it does with children who move friskly, laugh loudly, and scream innocently.

You, my master, are penetrating within me like the pores of my body, intertwined to the point that it cannot be separated.

We can never realise their cohesion or their interdependence.

How wonderous is this bond that attracts you and compels you to leave the farthest point on earth and come to me.

It makes you yearn for me in my presence and absence.

How wonderous is this love that comes at a late age, and which is like magic or like a spell.

The more this love tries to get drunk, the more it gets thrilled, intoxicated and burnt.

It is very strange that this love makes your birth count from the moment your heartbeat beats for my love.

Your true lifetime begins the moment I glow inside you, the moment I sail in your seas without boats or oars.

So your hands will be my oars, and your soul my boat.

It is strange that this love erases all the years of your life, and makes you feel love this way.

Before now you have never loved.

Before now your longings have never committed suicide in front of a female.

Before now all your physiological functions has not worked. Before now you have never known the true language of love. Before now you have never known the homelands of true longings, the flowing rivers of love, and the true shores of your heart.

Before now you have not experienced a romance that makes you melt in the first meeting.

In every meeting there is a painting for eternal love that makes you as if you are born every moment, and emerge from your mother's womb, pure, holy, and pure.

You have never known that love also has its sanctity and purity. The heart and soul together dance at the advent of the dawn of love.

It will make you young at the prime of youth.

It will cancel all the rest of your life, as it is without a soul, existence, and a title.

You have never known that the world has love that will make you the sultan of the love kingdom.

It will make you a lover roaming through its realms.

This love will uplift you from these worldly territories to the sky and the celestial realms of the universe.

You have never known that one day you will be weak and strong in the kingdom of love.

You will have a princess who looks like the charming women of paradise, surpassing all the women of the world, and freeing you from the constraint of time and space within you.

You will roam with them in the parts of the earth, and choose for them a lot of new territories.

Perhaps you will choose the land of China or India or Persia as a beginning of your new love.

Indeed now, Sultan, I understood the romantic poetry of Qais.

I realized how much Harun al-Rashid loved women.

I grasped the love case that Nizar Qabbani had experienced, and the love stories of many others.

Thus Nizar's beloved was born, lived and immortalized in  verses of love to the end of time. Such verses were composed by a passionate lover and were made into a model for every lover in his time.

They remained as an example to be followed by all the successive generations.

Love is not always like myths.

Love does not always live like history.

It continues like civilization.

Princesses of love do not always exist, because one day, in some land, there will be only one sultan, and he will desire one princess.

She will continue to love him, she will grow in love, flirtation, praises, continuous infatuation, and hot yearning.

# 8

# I am waiting for you

There will be a vast land and a bright sun which he will be clothed in its light and wrapped in its threads.

He will be longing for her, desiring her, wandering with her, being alone with her at all times.

He will be stronger than anything that binds her to him.

However, she alone is his strength and weakness.

Look at him wearing his black coat, standing and leaning on the sidewalk fence in order to forsee his being with her at the distant horizon.

So, his heart can sing melodies for her, and say to her: "You have deprived my eyelids from sleep, hidden all my bed pillows, and lit all the candles of your femininity within me."

It is not the black coat that indicates his favorite color, but the red color is the motive of his search for you and your presence within him.

It is the only symbol that guides him to you.

The red color represented in his tie that he wraps around his neck is his desire for you and for all life.

He does not care about distances, times, places, not even ages, because he simply loves you, rather adores you, and desires you.

How long he would stand staring at the distant horizon.

Will he meet you one day?

Will you really be his, or will you remain like a mummy in the Pharaoh's palace?

Will you be just like a dream that is neither extinct nor present in reality.

He was always standing in front of the sea calling you and sending to you the sweetest and most intense feelings.

He used to tell you all his concerns that he did not tell to anyone.

He was passionate about your closeness, your love, your letters and your tenderness.

He wanted you at any price, because you are his whole treasure.

He used to stand looking at the distant horizon, waiting for your arrival every single night.

His age was forcibly taken from him because he always said, "My age has not been counted yet."

He was always waiting for your arrival at every sunrise, at every sunset, at every inevitable passage of seconds.

He always stood tall in his black coat and red tie, waiting for your arrival to take you to a table he had prepared on the balcony of his house in front of the sea, to light all the candles, and to present all the gifts he had collected for you throughout his life.

He would swear to you that he never loved a woman, other than you, so madly like this.

He would dedicate the rest of his life to you, to recite all the prayers of his love for you.

He was standing tall in his black coat and red tie, waiting for your arrival...

# 9

# That's how you are, O Pharaohs!

You see how feelings move you to flee to another world.

You thought that the mother of the world, Egypt, alone would contain you.

You thought that the Nile alone quenched you.

Yet, neither the mother of the world contained you nor the waters of the Nile quenched your thirst.

Your thirst was gone while you were searching for her everywhere.

You were searching for her beauty, tenderness and for her faint voice, like a quiet night.

I wonder what on earth forced you to head for her distant cities.

What made you leave the whole world for the sake of such silent beauty that lives in exile on the mountains, dwelling the heart of virgin nature.

She was once the most beautiful girl in her town.

She was the focus of everyone's eyes.

Her beauty fascinated everyone to the point that no one could resist it.

She was so lofty in her value like patriotism, and liberated like freedom itself.

She was as high and lofty as the date palms of the desert.

What tempted and attracted you to her, O Pharaoh!

For sure, you love to travel and roam through all the world and in the end you return to the arms of the Mother of the World.

This is how you, Pharaohs, like to dazzle the whole world in your land and outside your land.

You love excellence in everything in the land of the Mother of the World, and outside it as well.

Excellence was created with your first existence like a leech in your mothers' wombs.

What compelled you to go to her distant exile?

What attracted you to her charming beauty?

Is it a new theory proven to all the people of the world that there is a belle asleep in the arms of the mountains.

She deserves to be titled the second Mona Lisa.

What on earth pushed you towards her, and changed the course of the Nile with you, so you took your boat with wooden oars, sailing towards her island?!

Is your story true or is it fabricated like one of the stories of a thousand nights?

Do you wish to have it acted next season?

Do you wish to have it played, and dazzle the other theaters all over the world.

# 10

# What made you head for this belle's exile?

What made you head for this belle's exile?

Was it to liberate her from all the constraints of time that make her a prisoner?

Was it to clothe her in the pink robes of femininity?

Was it to adorn her with gold and diamonds?

Was it to dress her with agate bracelets and necklaces, and emerald earrings?

Was it to make her a princess on the Nile and the pyramids?

Was it to record her with you in the eternal history of mankind? You will decorate her fingers with golden rings, put anklets on her elbows that you brought from India on your last trip.

You will dress her in a red sari embroidered with precious stones.

You will cover her head with a transparent red shawl.

How did you know that she loved that color?

And she loved the sari with the jewelry and the anklets, whose sound indicated that there had been a distinctive luster behind that beautiful face.

# 11

# O pharaoh would that I knew...!

O Pharaoh, would that I knew how you fell in love with her!

And how could she attract you from all the world surrounding you?

How could she capture your heart and dwell in your soul like a swaying flower in its bud, caressed by the breeze?

How could she give you all this love and this pleasure?

How could she change the course of your whole life and force you to love her deeply, the same way you loved life before?

How could she grant you the happiness that made you a distinguished and happy Pharaoh who would fly from one plane to another and from one country to another?

How could she make you pledge all your life to her?

And how could she rob you of your buried sadness, and bandage your deep wounds with her eyelashes?

Would that I knew how charmed you her letters, her colors, her drawings, her voice, and the sparkle of her eyes!

How did all that happen to you?

## 12

# How could she free you from the silence of the years?

Would that I knew how she could liberate you from the silence of the years!

How could she kill cowardice in you?

How could she cancel all your travel trips to a life of misery once she got the passport to your vibrant heart and eternal love.

How could she kill the annoying and boring moments within you?

How could she turn your dull, monotonous life which was full of chaos into a dreamy, rosy and colorful life?

How could she revive the long-sleeping child within you for years, and take you to the whole world flying with her flock of love?

Who on earth has guided you to her exile?

And to her rugged roads?

She abandoned the whole world and stopped searching for you.

However, she fought all people to be with you.

She went through various experiences in which she tasted pain, suffered wounds and felt deep sadness.

She chose her exile due to the severe grief that people caused her.

She did not tell you anything about herself and she never wants to say anything.

She buried all her wounds in this exile.

She was hurt a lot, but when she saw you she forgot everything.

So, don't ask her about anything, just ask her about her love for you, and about her desire for you.

She wants you, only you and no one else.

She is preparing herself to be your only bride.

She is giving you new ages for free.

Before you, sadness and pain killed her, and resided a long life in her.

Almost all her beauty withered and all her letters had vanished with her.

She was sure that one day you would come to her kingdom and liberate her from the overwhelming sadness buried inside her and liberate her from the chains of bloody wounds.

She was sure about your coming to her to make her a princess who exceeds all the beautiful princesses of all monarchs.

She will be the most beautiful woman ever created on earth, because only God distinguished her with this beauty and this beating heart with your love.

Your alone made her unique among all the females of the earth.

# 13

# Congratulations on this love

Do not ask her about anything in the past.

She cannot remember anything but your love and your passion for her.

She remembers nothing but the continual beating of your heart, and the frisking of your beautiful soul.

She remembers nothing but your smiley face and your constant laughter.

She remembers nothing but your fragrant body odor.

She only remembers your warm embraces and your arms extended towards her to hide her inside you.

Do not ask her about anything, because she cannot remember the past except when you were in it.

She also cannot remember the present except when you are in it, or remember the future except when you will be in it.

She is your only belle who arranges your desk, writes your day's schedule, and brings cups of tea that you like to have while you are immersed in your research.

She will arrange all your books and stuff as she wants only your comfort.

Would that I knew what storm of feelings blew on you and took you away to her exile?

What on earth took you away to see her, to bring her with you to your beautiful kingdom, to put her on the dresses that you brought from various cities of the world.

The dresses which used to attract you whenever your eyes fell on them, and saw them as beautiful pieces of music adorning her.

You always thought about her, and would choose her stuff with great caution.

You would focus on everything you bought for her.

You wished that she would be the only woman to wear them.

You wished that they would be exclusive to her just as she was the only one who was exclusive to your heart and soul.

She also clothed you in the cloaks of happiness and contentment.

She made you a man who constantly proves his manhood.

She made you a distinguished prince.

What on earth drove you to her exile so that she would dazzle you with her beauty and delicate spirit, and awaken within you the feelings that had been sleeping for years?

To awaken the feelings that have never moved for a lifetime. The feelings that subsided and slumbered for long.

After that you did not ask about them and you did not realize why those same feelings inhabited you?

It seemed to you that life went on like that, but today you have found another world, another dreamy, strong and wonderful life.

Congratulations, O pharaoh, on this love and these glowing feelings!

And congratulations to her on your love for her!

# 14

# I don't know why you were submissive to fate

I don't know why you were submissive to fate. You were yielding and walking with a shivering heart that was talking to you about her. It was talking to you in private and publicly.

How unbending you were in conquering your feelings and wearing the coat of patience and silence!

How often have pens, books and all technology made you forget about innate life and divine feelings?

Indeed, you were working like a machine non- stop.

You were walking through the roads, streets and fields without noticing the divine beauty displayed in them, and without your sight enjoying them.

You were leaving from one place to another without your eyes seeing the splendor in it at all.

Pity on you, O Pharaoh, who was inhabited by silence and apathy for years.

You were gnawed by so long nights, and inhabited  by the bats of deep sorrows.

How great you were among people and in sciences!

How great you were in containing your wounds and sorrows!

You were great you were in wasting your happiness, though!

You could give happiness away to all people, but you could not give it to yourself.

# 15

# On your cheeks are silent gardens

There are silent and empty gardens on your cheeks.

Now, you are searching hard for my letter.

Before that you have been searching for my pulse, probing on my heart and asking it a thousand questions.

You are searching throughout my eyes for your palace, for your existence, and for my poetry that abandoned me.

You are asking about my devout worship in the sanctuary of your love.

You are searching for my sincere intentions of love.

You used to scrutinize everything.

You used to archive my feelings in an antique drawer.

You used to make up a thousand excuses for me to navigate into my silence, into the noise of my speech, in order to embrace my poetry.

I was not like now.

I said that all surging and revolting feelings will subside except those of your eagerness.

Revolutions will continue to fight for eternal love, for unceasing spirituality, for mastery of the so-called love languages.

However, I always convince you that love has only one language despite different places or times.

Do you see that all revolutions can subside except for the revolution of my spiritual heart that cannot subside or lose its track?

Your revolution can abstain from all the worldly things except for the fountain of your longing and love, for it is always thirsty.

I am the mystic in the temple of your days, waiting for the time when your soul trembles, looking for my journey in the ocean of your feelings that resound like the sounds of bombs and cannons in battles.

You are the only one who sweeps away time crawling towards me, and moves the stars that surround me.

I am asked about the light that is surrounding me, so I fear to tell them that it comes from the lights of your soul.

The lights that are fleeing from us both to non-existence... to nowhere.

# 16

# I am still seeking an eternal journey in your arms

I am still seeking an eternal journey in your arms.

I am traveling through your eyelids and recite in your ears the praises of the soul that has been tired of long travels.

The soul that days, volatile destinies and distances have fought.

I am a devout worshipper in the sanctuary of your eyes, repeating the praises of my heart pain that life has made it bleed.

My heart is being squeezed like a sole garment owned by a beggar who has been wet by rain.

I do not flirt with you, nor do I say false words to weave the brightest garments of feelings, but I adore everything in you.

I hesitate to tell about you as I hesitate to say the sacred words that a believer memorizes, and recites abundantly in his solitude.

Misery and hope have never met together despite the pain, but I have always been eager to meet you as a crawling baby, indifferent to everything around it.

You were and still are my hope.

You were like a prayer that I would constantly repeat because you were very exceptional.

# 17

# Don't tell me tales about love

Do not tell me tales about love because it is greater than all the words I hear from you.

It is much greater than the delusions of pens and papers.

It denounces the defilement of words and all human intrigues.

I found it like a vast universe in which you live but you can never appreciate.

I found my soul more comprehensive than all the confessions that we are forced in some situations to say.

I found that true love is all the words that we never reveal , but the words that we conceal in our hearts.

We refuse to let them come out of our mouths, that is why I do not want to read anything about feelings and eagerness.

For we do not master their languages, and we can never speak them.

We do not know how to formulate them and so our hearts are unable to understand them.

Excuse all the lovers when they burn with longing and cannot stand it, because it is impossible for love and distance to exist together.

For the one who is far from their beloved will never be crowned by patience.

A myth is everything that you say about what stirs our souls. The myth is everything you used to tell us about the dancing of hearts or even about their pains.

A myth is all the gossip and stories that were told.

# 18

# The fatal jealousy

I don't know why all the women are jealous with so much anger?

They get jealous of revolutions and inhumane rampage

They compel men to flee from them or move away from them instead of bringing men closer to them!

Why don't you make very peaceful wars out of jealousy?

Why not double her love?

Why not change the course of her life and make another human being out of the children of Adam?

Wherever he escapes, he returns to her.

Why doesn't she avoid equivocating him, because this is his nature?

I hate the jealousy of an ordinary woman and I hate her revolutions that always failed.

I hate the authority of a woman when she wants to possess a man and wants to control his mind, forgetting that she is liberating his heart for the sake of the new search journey.

She wants to possess him in her own way while she is outside the circle of his heart.

The heart is the only entity that guarantees you whether to stay or leave.

So, a woman must engrave herself, like a stone, in the heart of a man whom she loves to the point of death. She must dwell in his depth and penetrate to his mind little by little until she gets him drunk. If not, she would not blame the man when he would search for another woman to throw himself into her bosom.

# 19

## **Every day, I am away from you.**

Every day, while I am far away from you, I imagined that it was so many years ago.

The pains intertwined inside me and tied me to the hook of a skilled fisherman, pulled me into the unknown and it seemed to me that I would not see you nor hear your voice as long as I lived.

I found all the clusters of my tears are not enough for me to sympathize with my grief, my pain, my wound and my heart that supremely loved you.

I was crazy about the time of the unknown, and the ropes of loss.

How can I meet you, enjoy seeing you and be happy with you?

How can I live and continue in this bitter life without you?

How can this love be suffocated by life with such cruelty?

Love that gives us hope and pleasure, and fills us with peace and joy.

I wanted you to be like the wings of a strong bird, so that I could fly to you, so that I could visit you frequently and know all your news.

# 20

# Photo album

I went to my photo album, flipping through your photos, one after the other, and speaking to them in a sad tone full of grief.

I was forcing my tongue to speak.

You seemed to be more depressed, and to be in more pain than me.

I feared so much for you.

I feared that I could lose you.

I feared that you would be sad like me, that you would suffer the pain that would strip you of life and creativity and would paralyze your brain.

I feared for you from the deadly storms of love, and from the estrangement of your life as well.

For you really need strong love that gives you warmth and security again.

Determination is not that you apply hard labor to your body in order to forget your love and to reach what you aspire to.

As it is said, "In order to forget the pain of our souls, we must work with our bodies non-stop."

For this you have to create a balance with two equal scales.

O my sweetheart, how much I feared for you from sadness in the first place, and pain in the second place.

I feared for you from wound and loneliness.

I have forgotten all what afflicted me.

I forgot my sorrows.

I knew that there was no sorrow comparable to the grief of my beloved.

I am accustomed to sorrows and their consequences all the time to the point that they forced me to adapt to them and get used to them.

I am accustomed to living with pain.

However, I never wish this would happen to my beloved.

I thought many times of a way to save you from everything that would surprise you.

Suddenly, I knew then how much I had wronged you.

How selfish I was when I wasted your time, knowing that you adored me madly.

I made sure that our love had other ways than these ways that we would take as an excuse for our meeting.

However, I cannot be away from you for a single moment.

I cannot be away from hearing your tender voice with which I feel warm and safe.

It is impossible not to think about you.

It is scary and disturbing not to care about me.

When I am trying to evade a bad situation, I find myself in a worse one.

How much I talked to your images, and how much I saw joy shining on your face.

You never know, my love, how much I love you, and how you are to me like the breath that I take in.

Words fail me when I want to express my feelings to you.

So, I find myself in the midst of a violent storm that uproots all the parts of my body that cracks and starts to collapse.

# 21

# I used to watch you every night while you were up.

I used to watch you every night while you were up, writing like a lover, or researching the secrets of science and nature deeply, or working as hard as you had never worked before.

All this happened without seeing me.

I was counting the ticks of time, running fast while I was close to you.

When you would come to sleep, I would live with you, second by second, sitting by your bed and observing your heartbeat.

I would cover you with my beautiful robe, straighten your cotton pillow, contemplate your face, sail in it, dance with your breath, and admonish your eyelashes for not containing me, for not embracing my soul in the height of pain.

I would admonish your eyes which were strained by reading books and papers, without noticing my presence with you.

I would admonish time that separated us and made between us countries, seas, and long ages that we could not bear.

However I find joy enveloping my depths and assuring to me that you love me violently and remember me all your time.

The dear beloved is not the one we always live with, but rather the one for whom we carry love in our depths as long as we live.

The one we find occupying our hearts everywhere.

You were very quiet in your sleep, as you ever used to be.

You were like a spoiled beautiful child, smiling constantly in your sleep.

When you would wake up, you would turn your eyes on my angelic face and extend your arms to hug me tightly.

You would invite me to have breakfast with you on a table in the garden of the house.

You would offer me a beautiful white flower, then carry your briefcase and go quickly to your work.

Before that you print a kiss on my forehead, as a token of such a beautiful day.

22

# The suffering of being away

I was happy when the feeling of sadness, burning, longing and pain had left you.

You were afraid of separation and pain due to my being away from you.

You were afraid of losing me.

You were afraid that you would not see me, that you would not talk to me.

You were fighting your depths and your heart as a strong fighter.

Then I knew how much you were fighting.

How much you were torn apart between a heart that would love me so madly and a mind that would reject me so arrogantly.

I knew how you overcame all the obstacles that would hinder you from achieving your scientific ambition.

And how you would remove, with the help of God Almighty, the huge rocks that were placed as barriers in the way of your success.

How you would sacrifice much to reach the summit, to reach the top of the pyramid that you planned for one day.

However, this cursed heart did not follow your plan and rebelled against you this time.

It rebelled against the strict laws of your mind.

I saw sadness surrounding you again.

However, I saw strong perseverance for work encompassing you from every side.

Then I was afraid, my love, for your being torn apart, for your struggling with yourself, and for your distraction from achieving your success.

I never like to be the cause of all this.

There must be a fair way for everything.

I am the superpower that occupies you, so it will definitely not destroy you.

It will never kill ambition inside you.

I am not the one who causes chaos inside you.

I am just like time, like the beats of time and heart.

I thought a lot about our present situation.

There must be an urgent solution to end all these disputes.

My love is being torn apart.

My love is in pain.

My love has a wound that is bleeding.

Now I have to be smarter and stronger.

I have to be the wisest and most rational woman.

My exaggerated concern for him kills him.

On the other hand, being away from him kills him as well.

My exaggerated concern for him makes him distracted, not concentrating. There must be a way out to end all this baffling dispute.

I must liberate my love from all these pains and from this chaos that occurred to him, and changed a lot in his life.

I am sure that my beloved's will is invincible, and his determination will not fail.

I devoted myself to help you with all my will, determination and strength so that you would reach your goals, my love.

* 9 7 9 8 3 4 8 1 3 4 0 0 6 *